# Fire in the Marrow

Poems

William Crawford

NeoPoiesis Press, LLC

NeoPoiesis Press
P.O. Box 38037
Houston, Texas 77238-8037

www.neopoiesispress.com

Fire in the Marrow
Copyright © 2010 by William Crawford

All rights reserved. No part of this book may be used or reproduced in any manner whatsoever without express written permission from the publisher except in the case of brief quotations embodied in critical articles and reviews.

Fire in the Marrow Poems William Crawford
ISBN  978-0-9819984-8-0 (paperback : alk. paper)
   1. Poetry. I. Crawford, William

Printed in the United States of America

First Edition

**Cover Photograph:**
*Benjamin, the last Tasmanian Tiger, by David Fleay*

*For Kimberly Schlagel,*

*a pure light source in these new dark ages.*

# Contents

Foreword ...................................................................................... v
Fire in the Marrow ....................................................................... x

## Between the Mirages

By My Own Hand ......................................................................... 2
Bluebird Notes .............................................................................. 4
Mesa Verde ................................................................................... 6
Ringing a Bell's Neck ................................................................... 8
Eye Howls .................................................................................. 11
Drum in Bluegrass ...................................................................... 14
Of Pearls and Swine, and All Things Before ........................... 16
Gentling ...................................................................................... 20
Torn From the Willow ............................................................... 22
Fox Travels Light ....................................................................... 24
Graveyard Shift .......................................................................... 26
The River is a Mirror ................................................................. 27

## Movie Stars and Slaughters

Cielo Scenes ............................................................................... 32
Scars on the Raindrops .............................................................. 34
In the Shadow of Arrows .......................................................... 38
Grand Mal .................................................................................. 40
It Should Have Been a Symphony ............................................ 45
A Sustained Grace Note From an Empty Bottle With a
Forgotten Saint on the Label .................................................... 50

And the Sun Shining on My Face ......................................... 53
Condensed Elegance .......................................................... 56
Sciamachy and Shell Roars ................................................ 59
Tauromachy in a China Shop ............................................. 62
Two Requiems for an Almost Poet ..................................... 65
If There is a Light, It Will Find You ................................... 68


## The Vision and the Void

A Bullet for the Blind ......................................................... 74
The Vision and the Void .................................................... 78
With This Ash We Polish Jewels ....................................... 82
Swing Low Sweet Pendulum ............................................. 85
Van Gogh Should Have Been a Verb ................................ 88
Minor Keys and Places ...................................................... 92
The Weight of Human Stain on Wing ............................... 94
High Society ....................................................................... 98
Weakness or Obstacle. ..................................................... 100
Not Long for This World ................................................. 103
To Catch and Cradle His Crown ...................................... 108
In Connection With a Drowning ..................................... 114


Epilogue ........................................................................... 117

# Foreword

In the prologue to this volume, the poet writes: "There's a pure light source pulsing from her eyes, real and empyreal." That is as good an explanation as I can make of the sorcery that is William Crawford's talent, his luminous *exceptionalism*.

Many poets reach the cusp of the transcendent, and it is always miraculous to experience the transformation invoked in the self/reader at the very moment of such connection. If you think about it, with respect to most great poets in history we remember two perhaps three of their works. In years to come, it is firmly believed that such will not be said of this artist. Each creation stands obelisk alone, the narrative weave in each is impelling, he is vision driven. Or in his words:

> I hope I never run out of ways
> of describing to you
> these things I see.
> >    from *ByMyOwn Hand*

He need not hope, as readers fortunate enough to read this stunning compilation will readily see. Crawford creates unforgettable, aqueous supralunary scapes. To see these expanses and intimacies he imagines, is to immerse completely, to permit wave upon wave of exquisite original beauty, rarefied insight, and sublime musicality to wash over you, till you cannot remember life apart from this sea of tranquil splendours and agonies. The truths are that elemental.

This essence of primal elementalism may well explain his frequent references to the effects of Van Gogh upon him, both the work:

> The sunrises are quick
> they shatter shadow
> and splatter Van Gogh all over the windows.
> >    from *ByMyOwn Hand*

and the imagined frail, humane artist:

> I want you to know,
> your paintings still eviscerate me –
> pull my beating heart out through my anus,
> and if that isn't genius,
> I don't know what the hell is.
>
>から from *Van Gogh Should Have Been a Verb*

Much as Van Gogh 'dreamed his paintings and then painted his dreams', Crawford takes us through lush, imagistic tales, often dream-like in their ethereal wisps, and then he slashes with eviscerating reality. This brutal beauty bears down heavily upon us for we realize the intrinsic linkage, which bears the stamp of humanity's *definition*.

Thus we are incised and transported again and again, the heart overspills as the attempts, the destitutions; the partial resurrections to a Godless afterlife, the true deaths, all infuse the reader's bloodlines. Yes, by his own standard, Crawford is genius:

after the amateurs are dissected
after a bloody beating heart is not detected
and last rites are written
I shall offer my writing hand to one of these brave new Ophelias
lead her down to the secreted ballroom
with its looking glass dance floor
with its sea of swirling eyes
a vision and a void inside of each and every one
I shall show her the vaulted ceiling
painted with all the fiery colours of the womb
both sunset and swan in a slumberous lake
the single crack that occasionally lets some light in
and we'll dance,
with the graceful carelessness of children
until the ceiling fractures and falls
and the womb fucking wrecks it.
                         from *A Bullet for the Blind*

We are given three pathways of beholding in *Fire in the Marrow*. In *Between the Mirages,* he opens with a quote by Camus discussing the paucity of real images *to be* beheld and captured. This is what the poet vows *not* to do here, in words to a frigid viper of a lover.

>All I can do
>is promise to never write
>another poem about the moon
>
>a tin drum
>a crippled horse
>a piñata heart
>      from *Eye Howls*

There are images that cripple, that ravage ...

...and others that probe to equal depths, just different recesses of the soul:

a photograph of a marigold
warmly fingered and folded countless times
the wrinkles are dry riverbeds
where sincere rain once rushed
with a graceful rage
towards a strange sea
seeking inclusion
      from *Torn From the Willow*

We move to a world of "Movie Stars and Slaughters", and this is so important because Crawford is the quintessential poet-cinematographer. In *Cielo Scenes* (for Sharon Tate) the tragedy of the actress' horrific death is woven into the strains of her life projected behemoth-high:

the golden shamble beauty queen
scrambled and breathless
on the parlor floor

the ruby blister traces
framing flawless measurements
a hot blooded silhouette
hemorrhaging a voluptuous void


The reel ends, a new reel begins:

brave, sad Aguirre
the blue flame which once danced
quickly fading in his eyes
the hopeless weight of his heart
which continued to beat
all bloody and tribal
a mad, simple rhythm of survival
            from *In the Shadow of Arrows*


It is almost ekphrastic perfection, save the depths of emotional, sentient penetration.

Finally we move to the precipice of the absolute question: The Vision and the Void.
Here the modalities of exhumation, examination, and breaching the distance, challenges our very conception of existence, metaphysics, and ontological truths, revealing them as the lambent prisms they are as well as the prisons they could be:


Exhumed oriole, orange breast bloated with maggots
slowly turning to song.
Fresh hell, unattended, a frieze of hungry eyes
slowly turning to snow.
            from *Swing Low, Sweet Pendulum*


To close on a telling anecdote: in a recent exchange about a work, Crawford was horrified at the suggestion his work was so 'beyond' that it assumed a 'sacred distance'. This is anathema to this poet. He tears open his core, and willingly opens himself to the reader. He lives to communicate, to touch. Another poet commented on the impress of his work, "[t]here are no functional substitutes for honesty, careful observation, and the reciprocity of kindness. We paint ourselves into limited frames when we are afraid to care and cling to a small corner because of our terror of flying."

Through Crawford's honest, observant, and ineffably kind eyes, we care. Through his pen, we fly.

~Constance Stadler

# Fire in the Marrow

Breakfast with the poetess, she's skinning an orange with fingernails bitten down to quick half moons. The sound it makes is a luscious alarm; it wakes me up faster than the strong black coffee I'm forcing down, chasing the taste of burnt bacon. Now she's breaking yolks, dipping wheat toast and avoiding eye contact. Envisioning her head in an oven, inside a quaint country kitchen with rooster curtains, the sun late to rise; everything going robin's egg blue before the bright white fade.

She tells me she's through writing for humans, about humans. She's sick of sucking at the bone, trying to get at the marrow, wondering if it tastes like fire. I tell her she should break those bones, create a mosaic with the fragments, enjoy life in the cool shadows of vulture circles, maybe write a story about her ex-lover Michael. How that jet plane crashed down on his street two days before he died. The dark roaring eclipse, then the new sun detonation that dominoed the row homes; razed beautiful post-modern ruins. Mothers baptizing fire-branded babies beneath cold, free-flowing hydrant streams; soft eyes forever changed, crushed into wide diamonds by the descending emergency. Diaphanous summer dresses torn and frayed from the shoulder, fiercely flapping flags of surrender. New ashen Joan of Arcs, seismically shaking, waltzing on a fault line, bracing for the aftershock – Munch scream scenes – a series of stills from Hiroshima. The drunk pilot's last words eternally preserved inside a black box, as insignificant as the prehistoric spider fly's frozen repose in amber.

She meets my eyes when she hears Michael's name, drops her fork, her act. Her cherry red mouth twists, twitches like a cat struck cardinal's death yield; now there's no eye shield, no distance between us. A fawn drawn to the head-lit highway, she sees herself on a star-crossed sign, she surrenders. And I love her, love the way she finds strength in vulnerability. She opens up, shares secrets from her sleeping depths, but she's awake not asleep; ejecting the darkness like squid ink, which writes itself on solid air.

She speaks for the first time of Michael's death. How she found him jackknifed on the bathroom floor. Pale skin mapped with purple veins, a sad savage cartography – her treasure stolen from his eyes. Red bandana still tightly wrapped around his right arm – a marked prisoner of a war with himself. The needle, the bullet that delivered the coup de grace – the sight of it always frightened her – still stupidly shining in a pool of Michael's vomit. He had left the water running into the tub. She unplugged it, listened to it drain, the comforting sound drowning the shock, calming her hysterics; it was like the familiar warmth of contact.

She placed Michael in the tub, closed his eyes, dumped ice over his disquietingly still body. She pushed ice cubes into his asshole, a cold resuscitation which she had read about in the Gram Parsons biography, and just like with Gram, it did not work. Michael was long gone, she couldn't let go. She removed her clothes and laid her naked, trembling body down over his, in the ice which felt like fire. She ran her long, lithe fingers through his hair; Kissed his eyelids, which she hoped had already opened up in a better place, improved by his arrival.

She whispered poems, songs, devotionals, entire breath penned bibles into his ears. She fell asleep in there with Michael. The ice snapped and thawed, while she hotly pursued him in her dreams; Spring vivid and twice as serene.

She ends the story there, takes our plates over to the sink. I walk over to her, she's not crying, she's just staring out the window. Perfectly still except for her heartbeat, which I can feel without touching her. There's a pure light source pulsing in her eyes, it's real and empyreal. I love them for all that they see, and all that they'll mean to me, come tomorrow. And I know she tastes the marrow, the fire it contains. I don't need to say it, I remain quiet, knowing words would just disfigure the moment – her becoming.

# Between the Mirages

*"A man's work is nothing but this slow trek to rediscover, through the detours of art, those two or three great and simple images in whose presence his heart first opened."*

*~Albert Camus*

# By My Own Hand

I miss sincerity.

I hope I never run out of ways
of describing to you
these things I see.

I envy the moon's drugged distance
a scythe too dull for the harvest.

\*     \*     \*

There's a canary in the mouth of the mine
she misses her cage, her song
the way the cat's eyes would bounce
and her heart would race
when they shared that space
filled with warmth and light.

\*     \*     \*

The sunrises are quick
they shatter shadow
and splatter Van Gogh all over the windows.

The crows discuss ideology
up on the highwire

obsidian abacus beads

Pasolini had ideas.

Who hasn't seen a telephone pole
and thought of a cross with themselves nailed to it?

A child preacher buried alive
by a bible black avalanche
which appeared as a hard sky falling

razors dripping stars down on impure elder skin

opalescent cumbuckets
milked by mothers
hand delivered

deliver us
from this thing
beyond good and evil

rain off eaves

this could be a leaving song

and if I had your face
you'd sing it to me.

\*        \*        \*

She said,
"no matter how fucked things are
the sky is always perfect,
the eyes of every animal,
sincere."

then she turned away shyly

and my mind preserved that moment
in fire, in gold

then she became some kind of timeless twilight
around her even the broken stuff shined

and I became weightless
suspended somewhere in her

not afraid to fall.

# Bluebird Notes

the headlights projected the road
the rumblestrips kept us awake
we took the river route
a serpentine fire road
listened to Bobby Timmons
moanin' on the radio

the river on one side
distant city lights and stars
brightly bouncing of its skin –
ghost lambency
a floating ballroom ceiling

the woods on the other
hissing blackjack trees
and wild blooming darkness
wood nymphs with voices like recorders
moon mad and luminous
naked and there for the taking
spread-eagled on evergreen altars

it's not a treasure once it's touched

we kept moving
and our minds reluctantly followed
knowing all dreams lack conclusion

we knew we were back in the city
when we spied a black-eyed feral child
skinning something beautiful
on the heat frayed median
then we watched a fountain
remake itself over and over again
youthful as spring

as a murder of crow-faced cops
descended on a gray, trembling man

skin like old newspaper – naked as sin
hung like a cashew

the twin stroke girls
stood there pointing and grinning
cyanide smiles
unaware that their beauty
would soon too blow a fuse

it was a sad scene
we took in the misery
now sick of motion
welcomed stasis
the urge to die young
even if we couldn't afford the funeral

to be forgotten
then remembered again
in moving sheets of indigo melody
in sustained bluebird notes
in standing applause
like hard clean rain

a round for us
and two for Timmons

his restless hands
knew this mood,
this feeling

all too well.

# Mesa Verde

I've never really thought of her as a beginning
but rather a means to an end.
There's a scar on her chin, it makes her self-conscious,
especially when it rains;
when I trace it with my lips,
unable to remember if I'm the one that put it there.

Sometimes there's a stillness in her eyes —
usually waxed moon wild —
faraway, like those enchanted painted canyons
I'd find inside textbooks as a child.
I loved sending my mind deep into them,
in search of lost magic, tiny cities of gold,
something to slake my thirst:
desert sand on sun-bleached bone,
a pox on the sky,
low vultures and turgid Morricone notes

floating away…

the thin skinned balloon of youth,
formed by my own breath;
towards her out stretched hand –
her pained smile –
a new wounded horizon –
I'm sure the world ends there.

But this stillness that softens her eyes –
it's a sudden stabbing stability.
I see sleeping mares in there,
tranquil lunar seas,
hear echoes from the womb;
the harmony of breath and heartbeat,
the smell of hot rain on honeysuckle –
sweet as rabbit's breath,
the cool green burst of wild cilantro –
a voluptuous line of flamenco dancers

which suggests the shape of her body.
She smiles painlessly for me.

I could hide in there,
inside her eyes, behind her hair.
I could die and go to soft hell there;
while she remains stoic –
a statue waiting for her Pygmalion –
a lachrymal to catch the tears
and the rain…
always on cue,
waking up the scars,
blurring the lens,
softening the dream
it hardly captures.

## Ringing a Bell's Neck

I felt these changes first in my inflamed limb

now useless and ruined

a soldier torn and frayed

encroached upon by

this rippling blue emptiness

which too

seems wounded


taking my teeth to the grenade's pin

only to chip olive drab paint

desperately wanting to dream

to weightlessly levitate

my way out of this wretched trench

which smells like death in summer

left neglected


and all of these tympani explosions;

the panoply of air raid siren voices

suggesting paper rectums, tigers;

silence seems distant, sacred

when the pin is pulled

and the tiny dancer spins

will the music box tell you

in notes that tremble

the way anxious trees do during shouts of TIMBER

that London bridges are falling down

for some fair lady again?

just like the green Parisian rain

in harmless exacting blades

that wish to get deep beneath your skin

as deep as your beauty will let them

as for me

I'll never find that dream

catch my breath, that cloud,

be (holy) wholly consumed,

consummated by another woman's womb

a new mother with soft eyes

honey breath and hollows

just deep enough to hold me

keep me for a while


how can I lean against

the blueprinted architecture

of my own dream –

moving like reverse fires

until the crutch cremates itself –

when I'm already a passive participant

in somebody else's?


a stranger with the lightest hair

and the darkest appetites;

a penchant for destruction and laughter.

# Eye Howls

I remember
the night I lost you
in the long grass
not a single cut from those blades

could have used a scar,
a condolement card,
something that stings—
something to jog my memory
every time it rains

and all the freefall
blindfold brushfire games,
fenestrations and forbidden zones,
were just a way to delay
the ineluctable slide

a spectacle of vision
deteriorating into void
a large collapsing star
never to crest,
never to blaze,
in these beautiful
razed ruins.

Soon new hands will find you
and work hard to redefine you

jeweler's hands…

the light goes out
you shine in the dark
with the dark

you've always had
a cross viper in your heart
and a frigid star in your chamber.

All I can do
is promise to never write
another poem about the moon

a tin drum
a crippled horse
a piñata heart

it would rather fall silently
and without pity
then continue to be beaten
brutally like this.

(an idiot's guide to writing the night sky)

I need to find
a fair game of Russian roulette tonight
because I'm in a Johnny Ace kind of mood.

I need to become a ghost
that broods,
that haunts,
that blooms
inside the mirror,
inside your eyes

and all the other places
where you worship
yourself as a flame
that can never tremble
like a flower

or cauterize a wound
in this wild blue hour.

Still, I assure you,
there's a pledge
waiting to be made,
a ballad
waiting to be played,

as soon as the needle
finds the groove…

until then
each click is
a heart palpitation
and a grave disappointment.

## Drum in Bluegrass

never mind these alabaster cygnets
that seem to swim by
on languid lapping waves of firewater

their distinguished crests
and fuse blown beauty
betrayed by black dahlia smiles

the crooked cockleshell shine
and resultant hard shadows
long and disenchanted

breaking diamonds
trapping flash frozen foxes
racing crystal rockets
behaving like graceless gazelles
out on a graze
while starving lions die young

your hands are better off
on their own
when they shiver and shake
like slashed veins

ache to paint a new scene
heal a crisp leper
steal an open-ended dream

or simply touch
that concealed hip flask of whiskey
and realize it's still half-full

you see
there has to be a painless way
to watch the gaze drunk sun
go fetal on the horizon

to find numb comfort
in the worn out appearance
that twilight confers onto everything

verdigris on an antique
crow's feet on your cheek
that damn lonesome sound
the bullfrogs make

sad as that pair of silver espadrilles
someone left hanging off the side
of this fire-forged bridge

they're the only things
that shine at this hour

almost new
yet already tethered
to a uselessness
that we shall all know
in time.

## Of Pearls and Swine, and All Things Before

she unfolds the mirror into a triptych

paints herself onto it

spread out

a baby bird frozen in her motion

she knows not the price of flight


the sun too close

set to wrinkle untested flesh

a voluptuous grape becomes a wizened raisin

knowing too much perfection

is a mistake

knowing her inheritance

is negligible without the wind

grounded in this beautiful bower

where the cool relief of shade

always ebbs –

a shy lover


when her breath darts like this

excitedly – the way a child breathes while dreaming

her rib cage collapses like an accordion

after a fitful tango

her tiny breasts have Bosch beaks

and seem out of proportion with her frame

which yearns to have its flames smothered


there's a song sewn in her ear

it taps her tin cochlea

she sighs deeply then tells me

another poetaster is in love with her eyes

as she adjusts her merkin

which she says reminds her of

said poetaster's goatee

and I'd agree if lice and crumbs were found

squirreled up in it –

dead fruit flies


there's a grain king from the plains

he's never seen the sea at night

or his mother naked through a bright keyhole

he's offered her a ring or something


there's a lute she has never played

propped up against her vanity

it aches to say something true

to be of use – to know her touch

there's a bucket of ice beside the bed

it snaps and loses its shape


I'd love to give her a baby

sire a child that could communicate with the dust

which never replies to my questions

though I keep asking


it's times like these

when her tears pool up all pregnant

fall in garlands of pearls

letters from some forgotten alphabet

descending without a sound

until they leave her face

and stitch the eager barrow

all pretty-eyed and hopeless

at her feet

always at her feet

which stink like the garden

and all the things she buried there.

# Gentling

I.
on days cancelled by sour mash bourbon
(helps keep the hands steady)
her daddy breaks horses
in the roundpen behind the silo
it's quiet there
the light bends softly
throws agreeable shadows
calm and peaceful
over time he has learned
you need these things to break them, properly.

accept the saddle
accept the bridle
accept the mount

he misses his little girl
her hand almost too delicate to hold
his hand calloused, scored by lasso,
stinks of lucky strikes and English leather
over her mouth
her smarting eyes widening
pooling with tears.

she developed early
hips like a lyre
voluptuous in body, in mouth,
just like her mother;
rest her soul.

he still tastes a little bit of her
when the bourbon stings.


II.
she's a poor mount
she won't let me take her on the bed

she won't let me turn the light down
prefers it rough on the hardwood floor
she slaps, she spits, she tells me she hates me,
her nails tear into my shoulder blades
she threshes and flails
bites herself, bites me,
this tragically beautiful creature
caught in a trap
beneath me
a snapping wildfire set to spread.

she cums and she cries
for what feels like an execution hour
she gets up and leaves me there in her room
I get up, collapse into the bed and wait,
sore and almost broken,
for her to return.

she returns
fresh and still naked
she could be a photo of spring snow.

she's holding a globe
a gift from her daddy
inside it a frozen rose
and a dry monarch
wings still as a sleeping horse
still as her daddy's hands
after that first morning bourbon
by evening restless and ready to wander
touch heather blossom tender flesh
he helped form.

she smiles gently
she shakes the globe
and nothing changes.

# Torn From the Willow

a photograph of a marigold
warmly fingered and folded countless times
the wrinkles are dry riverbeds
where sincere rain once rushed
with a graceful rage
towards a strange sea
seeking inclusion

a faded sun
set to shatter on the bold horizon
brightly burst with new birth
a beautifully formed daughter
whose radiance is willing to bend
contort itself so that it touches the darkest corners
washing them brilliant
as the shadows Munch scream and dissipate

can you still see the Lüscher bruises
that sharply ache beneath this breath catch beauty?
that wish to inherit a trade wind
press your hand to her belly
there's a sea change
feel a kick that tests for echo
and it's ok if your hand shakes a little
and it's ok if the answer is late returning
for now this is home

yes, it can begin the way a dream ends
stretched across this wondrous distance
coruscating with newness
with all the honest colours of fire
soft autumn parades and fanned smiles
matching eyes and wings now tested
mended by a wind
that remembers you
as a precious thing
torn from the willow

we can draw our own conclusions
in song and in sonnet
on the bleeding red wall of a heart
we almost pawned – in haste
guided by a worthless hunger

we can touch this
and still call it a treasure
we can release it
and be certain of return.

# Fox Travels Light

There could have been a new swan-necked Juno
beneath the thinning veneer of that pale blue pool
a popping lung, a lazy eyed surprise,
the spastic gasp of a sudden entry, re-entry
before it all ices over again, catches the sun all wrong
revealing sheets of Braille,
hardly as bright as Rouault's ancient oils
or the slow motion crumble
of frigid star constellations
construed as carbuncles, treated with mercury,
freeze and watch this atrophy
graceless figure 8's and the sharp flinch
of an ill-knit scar
as it remembers itself, us too, too soon –
measures us in discounted rain
never straight or true
still we drink it down and continue to feel empty
the void never glistens.

Were you ripened on dog-strangling vine?
did you wipe out every last wildflower?
poison the soil,
all of those stories stymied by your hideous strength,
they once steeped and rose up like dreams there
until you pricked that thin skinned balloon
wire-hangered that infant-eyed dream/womb
now it's all just the bright garland of dead honeybees
stinging nothing in the muck and mud
a souvenir, a savage thread of your easy nihilism
dark as your eyes –
the Mesa Verde on a three coyote night
surely whore's dream cold.

Howl. Howl. Howl.

Over stolen boxed burgundy wine
under a plugged-in sun, skin turning orange,

we sang our ballads
both relevant and irrelevant
equal part sybarite and philistine
and after the seventh sign
in memory of black and white
you passed for pretty
full and pale –
Gwathmey's autumn bouquet
a slightly bruised arrangement.

All that heat mirage motion
and swirls of spilled tiger's milk
a debutante's awkward first facial
the Comanche laughter of the camera –
a loud, stupid war whoop,
rather than the quiet harsh truth –
a frangible halo in her eye
soon to shatter
in blocks of vague space
in dense tangle of tongue;

she almost passed for poetry.

I see full on night here
parallels of the fox
a noble, clever beast
with a racing heart
she always travels light
dips her swift paws
into the gore
of the animal she wounds
runs red circles around trees,
throws the hounds off her trail;

cunning, beautiful creature
the hunters sleep tonight
your freedom, a stranger,
known only to them in dreams.

# Graveyard Shift

when transcribed the dialogue was so small
one could only read it through a microscope
with a naked eye
twitching like a dying fish
punctured by the screaming hook
big bloated eyes of blue
sadder than the spider veins on mama's legs

double shifts at the diner
where the weak neon glows 'til dawn
and the talk is always small
silverware glockenspiels ringing plangently
nicotine swans and black coffee blues
muleskinners on the jukebox
waitress breaks a nail

they'll bury mama here
on company time
no music, no elegy
just the mindless murmur
of dead end dialogue

coffee stains and liver spots
wizened wallpaper
and a slow glowing clock
with hands that could never understand
what it's like to cherish and to hold
or relinquish without regret.

# The River is a Mirror

she could be a sacred deity
lissome and glistening
out there in the river
which, today, looks like a mirror
and when the sun touches the skin
tests the tensity of the soft surface
it all catches fire

the waves become tongues
seem to dance straight through her
rise in distinguished crests around her
a flaming tableau
it rises in propinquity
with your blood
on the distant shore
ignited by this divine cynosure
the language is music
it flows effortlessly
with its own languid, pellucid poetry

and you know
her almost flawless shape
could never be formed by human hands
with ancient clay from the riverbed
which silently holds every lost story
until end merges with beginning
in fiery kiln, or watery womb
no, she was born again today,
born for you,
now worship

see how
the sun has already turned her skin
brown as the great Ganges
burnished her hair
gold as jute

hear the music
in each of her movements
the exotic rhythms and scales
beguile the western ear
the same way
her incandescent beauty
leaves its indelible mark
on the western eye
continues to flash
first red then silver
elegantly rimmed with shadow
long after the eye has closed

remember last November's Diwali
a festival of lights
the heavens touched earth that night
walking through constellated gardens
moving through several milky ways –
horse head nebulae
Tantalus no longer denied by distance
permitted to touch
a softness he could never imagine
a beauty impossible to define
an elaboration of his own passion
the longing he measured in ash
the dream no longer a burden

she danced for you that night
your own private swan lake
she had the innate grace and danger
of a charmed cobra
held in the pungi's rhythmic sway
Kali veiled by stars

you sat and watched
wondered about the palaces in her eyes
the bright flights you had missed by mere moments
all the places you had never been to
you were an entranced outsider, a lucky tourist,
held to a promise in her eyes

legs too weak to dance with her

now she's here again
reborn in this river
bright eyes blooming lotus
all peacock and bell

beads of water and sweat
twinkling jewels on her elegant neck
breathing swans and songs
as she turns gold at sunset
your blood could only riot
until it spatters itself into sonnet
pulsing on parchment
all red and untamed – palpitating –
a bengal tiger's heart

and when she's gone
don't feel bereft
don't remember her
as a mortal or a goddess
just think of her as a place of rest
a place where your heart first opened

name this river, this mirror,
after her.

# Movie Stars and Slaughters

*"Too much perfection is a mistake"*

*~Alejandro Jodorowsky*

# Cielo Scenes

*for Sharon Tate*

remembering those cielo scenes
the Christmas lights and spilled wine
on August's altar
built for the snow queen

the boys that once spelled her name
with lit sparklers in the dark
now off tearing wings from butterflies
losing ten pace shootouts with the stars
to keep themselves from mourning
to forget the slow blink
of those flash bulb shocked eyes
every time they close their own

the lawn was littered
with strange new starlings
and fire sale garments
a tinsel lasso of damselflies
dead in the pool

sapphire gin
and a record skipping –
stoned into oblivion

the golden shamble beauty queen
scrambled and breathless
on the parlor floor
the ruby blister traces
framing flawless measurements
a hot blooded silhouette
hemorrhaging a voluptuous void

a cat-calling, wolf-whistling darkness
quick to encroach
consuming the room
cancelling the mirrors

shake waking the dream

savagely kissing
her crushed wild strawberry mouth
from an anxious distance –
a precious redbird you can't touch

aurora borealis eyes and aura
long gone

loosen the rope
let her go
from gilded cage
to open window

with no memory
of this slaughter.

## Scars on the Raindrops

the timing was always bad

a dago red window

hemorrhaging heat

petechial scarlet spring

both Venice and Vienna


a glass eyed doll

limp on a balcony

suggesting scenes

dreamed by Fellini


Christmas lights

startled by the depth of their own blues

blinking in early May

waiting for the late darkness to descend


damn this mirror as it shatters

as you open your arms again

hoping for a song this time

comparing common scars

on the raindrops

off-white and awful

set deep in azure


she blew songless bluebirds

out of the right side of her mouth

from the left

she blew penny wishes

blew haloes and grace notes


eyes so still and steady

unblinking

as she gave that confession

to you

her camera


she was quite the actress

her face exquisitely lit

on one side

the softness of shadow

on the other


a gentled moon

clair-obscure

that long flowing jawline

a dangling dolichoid dancer

her mouth a beautiful wound

a strawberry roan

ready to run


and you wished

she would blink just once

just close her eyes –

both blue flower and flame –

allowing rest

possibly dreams


her body was a limestone cathedral

and yours

a snake willing to swallow

anything before it.

## In the Shadow of Arrows

the birds are quick to follow you
crestfallen and songless
for they know how it feels to swallow stone
and this promise is too easily broken

a salt-wound sky
a savage omen
this must end with ignominy

the word sorry –
the sound it makes on a tangled tongue
well, isn't it really just
a single hand clapping?

an implacable brat
that spits upwards at the sun
that hisses at snakes
already snapping in the fire

-silence-

and when you finally meet your own eye
take time to survey the hollowed out galaxy
once mistaken for a lost city of gold

fasten your restraints
for this collision of vision and void

mirror martyrs barter breath for paper gods

-numb surprise-

pity poor Aguirre
his beautiful delusions
his spurious map of El Dorado
his tiny raft overrun with barking monkeys

set to sink
anchored to a dream
that rushes into blind depths
deaf to the tragic music
the operatic chorus of goodbyes

brave, sad Aguirre
the blue flame which once danced
quickly fading in his eyes
the hopeless weight of his heart
which continued to beat
all bloody and tribal
a mad, simple rhythm of survival

even in the shadow of arrows
poison dipped and dead aimed.

# Grand Mal

I.
measure the length of this division
and the subsequent disrupted scenes

before her face split in two
both sides equally beautiful

just as exquisite as the flaws
this intimate camera,
too close for comfort,
always seems to isolate

not to exploit
rather to study
and then celebrate

in remembrance of halcyon moments
where motion was created
only to be suspended
in some kind of weightless surrender,
elegant surrender.

II.
remember the day,
not the same as those before,
that strange feeling –
of flint sparking brightly inside

imagining some approximation of fire –
as if it was promised

when she took you down
to that shattered stone beach

a battered old soul
a sadness which revealed the density of your bones

and that crash, it frightened you,
made you second guess her intentions,
the message your own blood
was urgently pounding out to you

just the restless surf
then an exhausted hiss
before the silence expressed all of it
all the things that never passed her lips
coyly parted as they were.

III.
she told you about the others
she had taken on the rocks,
naked in the sea

measuring the words carelessly –
as if to wound you

and you prayed it was all
just a dispassionate play

a mechanical act,
an animal act,
profoundly meaningless

and you hoped
she wasn't irreparably torn

because in your mind her eyes seemed dead
when sewn inside those vicious scenes
the way they stared back at you,
into you,
saying nothing
as strange tongues
danced in and out of her wounds –
the kind only a woman knows.

IV.
was she not both tragic black dahlia
and beaming cheshire?
one side smiling,
the other howling

shivering in the terrible sunlight
and you felt it strange
her shivering that hard in the sun
and you wondered was it really just the sun
making her shiver so seismically

that sick pink sun
a hostile contagion
which made her skin seem too pale –
almost translucent

her neck too long and exposed
tirelessly pulsing
her lips swollen and almost ugly

two beautiful faces fused together
into something vaguely familiar
yet palpably grotesque

you had no choice
but to recoil
all the while cursing the sky,
your own Judas eyes.

V.
later on
further down the beach
you sat on the rocks
the gulls streaming and screeching
as you watched the waves
breaking around her

she wore the water
like a gown of jewels

and when she slipped it off for you
you knew it was better to stay a stranger
to such impossible beauty.

VI.
sudden night
found her taking another stab at becoming light
opening her eyes,
revelations in their whites,
opening her wrists,
through fat that glistened
down to humming bone
a crooked line of teeth
in a collapsing coal mine
before the great black catastrophe

descending heartless
abattoir darkness
a wind which whistled
an executioner's song.

VII.
you leaned against the dream too long
a crumbling crutch –
a malformed thalidomide limb

sad eyed albatross
deconstructed holy cross
mountains and their grand mal seizures
head first into the sea

ring in the new Pompeii,
same as the old Pompeii

the big sleep promised easy tourism
so you followed her there
she left a trail of broken nimbus
she left her cloying scent
heavy as fire lily

you were numb and lost
in her final set of frames

the camera zooming in so close
capturing you in her eyes
one for each face

and for something like a second
you were home,
improved inside of them

then the camera panned away…
revealing skull and peacock,
penis and broken window,
on the periphery;

the sound of water dripping

then, all too soon, it did return
back to her
just in time to catch her final act
mouthing the word, "nothing"
before the screen went bombazine black.

# It Should Have Been a Symphony

Woyzeck tried to carve a new sky

with slow dazzling guts

a blood red bird of carrion

a set of lazy voluptuous lips

slightly parted

ready to spill a secret

or fulfill a promise

Man Ray would later see this

with one eye open

on the great wall

of his mother's womb –

spend an entire lifetime

trying to recreate it.


A man sometimes constructs a gabbia around his soul

a perceived vulnerability

a cage of wrought black iron

more a trap than a defense

*osteogenesis imperfecta*

unprotected from the lycanthropic wind

the soul howls along with it

wildly it swings

starving for protection

space and division

crippled as it is.


Woyzeck turned back his eyes

stared

a cold naked stare

into an abyss

which made him dizzy

with the sound of locust

the stench of pestilence

he weaved a sad waltz along the precipice

before plunging into full-on endless night

starless and shamed

the faithful sting of savage memory.

That beautiful whore Marie

dancing gracefully

dangerously

and happy

cheek to cheek with the drum major

those exquisite cheekbones

on high with a smile

dimples dripping mercury

to cure his syphilis

*"I'd rather have a knife in my body, than your hand on me", said Marie*

sad sweet Marie

with her chestnut hair swept up off her shoulders

that lone mare dark as night

loping in her eyes

turning away from Woyzeck

running away from Woyzeck

leaving his heart broken and degraded.

The sky slowly turning to ash and cinder

festering red in the sun

barely reflected off the pond's ancient skin

blood letters on butcher paper

a wounded eye

a craven voyeur.


Woyzeck's blade whistled Schubert not Beethoven

as it descended deeply into Marie

*Der Tod Und Das Madchen*

Marie didn't hear it

she only heard the susurration of the willow tree

weeping its fare thee well

or was it the grief struck grebes

finally taking flight

all at once

the sound they made

with their narrow wings madly beating –

a solitary gunshot.

The pond's skin rippled just a little

before it swallowed

the knife

still hot and ringing

silently

Woyzeck followed.

## A Sustained Grace Note From an Empty Bottle With a Forgotten Saint on the Label

*for Wm. Holden*

The golden boy claimed the crown early in the game
Bogie told him it was the softest racket in town

god, he hated that bastard Bogie
with that slanted smile and toupee full of camphor

"to see how far I could lean without falling"
ironically he once said this

"hell is paved with good Samaritans"
he didn't say that, another Wm. Holden did,
but he sure would have appreciated it

when his resplendent realism dimmed
when the silver screen was pawned
for thirty easy bits

at cut rates
in the precarious shadows
by hucksters all rheumy-eyed with avarice
to soi-disant, powder burned street hawks

he sought numb comfort in solitude
the right to remain silent

there are reasons why a man drinks alone
there are reasons why a man prefers to be left alone

things that are better left unsaid
things that slowly murder the mind
the conscience is often a blunt instrument of torture

he died alone, hidden

without human stain compromising dignity
the way all noble tigers prefer to

safe from the poacher's obdurate blade
its dull backward lesson
its lack of reflection

his only audience in that seaside high rise
a stoic, fragile line of Japanese figurines
a frieze of staring eyes
smoky, distant, dour
with no relief in sight

he leaned too far
crown shattered in that great collapse
with no one to catch or cradle it
no one heard that impacted echo
no one felt the seismic aftershocks

he bled out
thin high proof blood
a sickly trickle first
if only for a moment
then a furious torrent

they found him four days later
motionless and tumescent
hardly the handsome actor they all remembered

it was not unlike that opening shot from Sunset Blvd.
face down in an exquisitely backlit pool
flashbulbs bursting like hothouse flowers
like the foudroyant marquees that shouted his name
that made passing crowds take pause

by then he was already removed from the scene
deeply dreaming of his spring picnics with Audrey on the Seine

his late summer safaris with Stefanie
through the sun burnished, russet wilds of Kenya

reflecting his own light
it was still golden there
the reality still resplendent.

# And the Sun Shining on My Face

*for Rocky Dennis as played by Eric Stoltz*

Rocky should have been a lion
his heart's beat, his mama's voice,
tells him just as much;

as he sharply impresses his bright dream cartography
onto the worn out soul of Europe.

he has triples of the '55 Brooklyn Dodgers
he has a winning suit, crisply pressed, mint julep cool,
inside the fridge.

he has simple solutions for life's hard equations;
no helmet when quicksilver daydreaming
on the restless side of this customized Harley.

\*\*\*\*\*

here she comes,
that tall blind blonde, Rocky knows, she's more than pretty;
her smile foments soft parades and riots in the blood.
and the tragic Braille of his face
is only a friendly stranger to eyes turned inward
and all of that true, natural beauty they are bound to find.

Rocky teaches her the relevant colours, the new sensations,
the effortless poetry of touch,
too much of a gentleman to introduce her to purple;
he lifts her hand, she touches cloud, understands billowy.

she touches his face too, imagines a softer Adonis,
and when they kiss on New Years
her tongue melts like cotton candy in Rocky's mouth…
they'll always have New Years.

and this memory, for Rocky,
it is sun shattering the ocean into rhythmic waves,

into luminous sheets of soft, uncut rain;
her face silhouetted in some kind of carnival light;
a light that only she could be the source of.

her loping equine jaw line
flawlessly framed by radiant, gilded storms,
by honeyed tendrils;
her exquisite lineaments
a tell-tale sign that a graceful god does exist.

*****

Rocky reaches for her, a dream much too real
to be leaned against for long.
she's gone but her summer redolence lingers –
he can taste it, palpable – discernible,
it's all dry heat, all swallowed sand stuck in his gullet –
just like the painful, bitter sting of this mask;
its permanence plays hideous tricks on the soul,
the same way their watchful eyes do.
Rocky wishes that this distance
could work like an effective Benzodiazepine,

but it doesn't; it can never be that simple,
so now it's all about Katmandu or bust;
and all the Silver Bullet Band songs become relevant,
become poignant, in the hard face of this.

still there's some softness in these tiny, fleeting moments
where Rocky watches mother gently hand feed
a rock dove; she moves so gracefully on that swing,
the sound it makes, a subliminal trigger,
it hastens the endorphins,
it ignites easy smiles.

*****

that final scene
it always gets me, Rocky

the way her hand trembles
as it raises the shade.

the indifferent cars speeding by
as she wraps the blanket around you
cocoons and merges you,
for eternity, with that dream;
a dream that pushes air,
that lifts masks, and drops armor.

she holds you,
knows you are still there,
knows you are everywhere.

and she says,
"now you can go anywhere you want, baby"
her eyes wounded, but not ruined,
still open; still searching for a reason to believe.

# Condensed Elegance

*three odes to three actresses*

I. *Barbara Leigh*

It was in an old-time rodeo movie with Steve McQueen,
that was the first time I saw her face
through windblown dusty vistas
she was surely the cynosure

the world stopped, exquisitely framed,
elegantly suspended
and my heart seemed to stop too,
as it opened in her presence

realizing she was her own event,
an elaboration of Indian summer
lingering with its own sweet electricity,
lighter than air,
with all of its lush promise;
its granted reprieve for newness and beauty

I was just a young boy
caught in her parade
of raining deciduous sunshine
catching her radiance in my eyes
I felt first time coyotes howling in there
I felt a song stuck in my throat,
realized it was just my heart
beating out sonnets to her

I waited eagerly for her next frame
for my marrow to be ignited
by her flashpoint physiognomy
knowing quite well it was the duty of the light to find her
and gracefully depict her, for she was its purpose

and now, thirty years later,
she's still more beautiful than ever

and my heart still opens in her presence
she swarms in, with the sweet purpose of bees to the honeycomb,
with a warmth all her own,
and I am captured, once again, in her golden scenes.


II. *Julie Christie*

I've seen her eyes before me many times
always forgetting that they are under glass

the warm, wondrous distance
between child and ferris wheel

twin sapphire prizes
eclipsing the sun

an easy deference.


III. *Laurie Bird*

She seemed too delicate
to be up there on that screen
with all of those muscle cars
and hard luck men
with that guileless smile
which suggested all things summer

eyes so wide with that softness known only in youth
she just seemed to glow
her bones just seemed to hum

discovered as a hitchhiker
few in years, breasts still small,
she had an innocence
like sunlight dancing on snow
gentle, pure,
a vulnerability that begged to be exploited,

and many other things
that are better left unknown

I sometimes wonder
what drove her to throw herself from that open window
if she somehow found a brave new mirror
in that sad defenestration

did the air quickly deduce the beauty
set to burst within her bones?
did she hum a threnody
during that scissor cut descent?

I ask the wind,
but there's no time for a reply,
it just sighs, remains faithful to her secrets

I can only hope it cradled her body softly,
held her for just a little while,
the way you are taught, at a young age,
to hold something precious,
something frangible and priceless;
always treasuring the touch.

but it's just a stage trick
and you bit

the crescendo comes
a clean tsunami crash

turns all bones to glass
shatters all the shallow seals and brittle symbols
you once held sacred

IV.
the hermit shell
was always yours to disown
was always more of a house
than a home

for you
it's useless now

but even at this new distance
if you listen close
if you relinquish fealty to the familiar
and fear of the unknown

you can still hear the ocean's waves
beating like your own heart
on your ear drum

that roar inside the shell
was always just an echo of your own.

## Tauromachy in a China Shop

when her brain feels bullet seared – wall splattered –
like Hemingway's final take on Pollock
and her thoughts ricochet through this rubber room
she leans with the shadows
as if to mourn
her pupils pinned

and the spotlight may as well be
a selective searchlight
it misses her every time

and the sand dips
i.v. drips
down that breath blown glass
soft as she pretends to be

the level of surrender
could almost be
a new, purer kind of pornography

then the sand catches her in the eye, in the act
it stings, it sparks, it makes her feel alive

it's a slow burning charge
it's tauromachy in a china shop
it's too tough for tears

she thinks:
must I keep skinning myself alive for this?

walks over to the three-way mirror
hoping that some part of her still sparkles
she'd like to see a blazing fire exit sign
she'd like to meet her own eye
but she won't, she can't,
no surprises tonight

she puts her face on there
another mask
another mirror
inside a dirt cheap motel room
dim Japanese neon
stiletto silhouettes
a beauty that presses too hard
blows a fuse

now she's out on the avenue
in the sewer steam slipstream
moving like an endangered feline
through gilded traps
and Darwinian rings of fire

blue smoke and gargoyles
spires that puncture the night sky
its filament thin skin
not unlike hers

she's a graceful geisha,
an untouchable bird,
a hangman's daughter,
she could give a flying fuck

she sees their famished alien eyes
all electric fire lust
inside the cars that cruise by
slowly, languidly, in soft focus

it all seems like a dream sequence
until one stops –

dig the driver's aviator shades
who the fuck does he think he is, Corey Hart?
buzz cut and a Village People wet leather cop moustache
marinated smile and execrable jazz leaking out of the speakers
real bad juju

she feels the heat

as his left hand motions
strangler's hand
ring finger tan line
he speaks perfectly clipped English
it sounds stupid – forced
community college crap
no place for it here

she pirouettes clumsily – a ballerina on valium –
and walks over to the pay phone
remnants of a happy meal smeared all over it
it stinks like crack baby shit
she nearly vomits as she pretends to make a call
imagining a pimp that looks like Venus Flytrap

Corey Hart rolls up his window
turns up the ac, the smooth jazz,
and merges with traffic,
with the night

she breathes a deep sigh of relief
catches her reflection in the chrome face plate
wonders what they see
knows what they don't

she places the greasy phone
back down into its cradle
lights a cigarette
just to watch it burn
all bright, beautiful and stupid
all the way down until it's gone.

# Two Requiems for an Almost Poet

1. Atomic Roses

explosions found him
all foetal and still
wrapped, somewhat warped,
in sheets of Shetland dream
the ground closer than ever before
wingless Pegasus still has pure slaughter value

the clouds didn't look atomic –
didn't look like magical hippie mushrooms
but rather holocaust roses –
a chthonic bouquet
for a frigid fishwife
hardly even cloud –
more like tattered shroud
stretched over herring's bone
pilfered of all silver
a kind of dim x-ray
all fracture and fissure

there was a lone raven
nailed to that curtain of secondhand gray
a tone poem bouncing off of her eyes
a sort of somniferous symphony or spell
soft and bright –
a hypnotist's pen

a moment of discovery
created just to be suspended
let us now lament
our inability to live within it

skeleton closeted in steaming depression
some skin still clinging to porous bone
the marrow cold and unfit to be suckled
dry scars on his arms

both crow trail and glory blaze
august rain falling with off-timed charisma
not unlike his own

there's blatant sorrow
in that hideous row
of exposed teeth
a pre-Cambrian skyline
or maybe just a jagged house key
unaware that the locks have been changed.

2. Finite Rush Hour Romance

his muse was ruined
by phallic devices (mushroom clouds, rockets, serpents, etc.)
cheap alcohol accelerated incinerations
his baited hook
forever submerged
in the Freudian slipstream
one day he caught his own reflection
and nearly drowned
in the shallows of himself

some student wet nurse
with hair like gutted virgin videotape
found him down in his green condition
successfully revived him with erotic C.P.R.

when he finally came to
she cleaned the spilled milk spangles
off of his pale blue irises
while he stared a single beat too long
the light was all wrong
it held a hideous secret
his face was his story
those lines –
a tragic history lesson she amended

she told him
that Freud was just a slippery mound of animal brain fat

that Jung was busy chasing after a gold rush –
which was really just his piss
being returned by an ill-tempered wind

moreover,
a broken window is rarely ever more than a broken window
and dreams often write themselves
even while they're dying –
forever is never an acceptable conclusion

he listened, wanted to drown in her

later on at the lakeside chalet
in the quiescent shadow of the mountain
she let him snort crystal ships
off the flaccid salt flats of her
waxed gibbous ass
all that white light, white heat,
the neutral bullets that would never know impact
chambered cold fire maids
feather-dusting the cobwebs from his brain

his heart stopped at that image
his face straight as St. John the Gambler's.

# If There is a Light, It Will Find You

I.
The Persian carpet makers had the right idea
the single flawed stitch
an errant star
a raw scar
obscene by naked eye standards

You see,
they knew too much perfection was a mistake
masterpieces made by human hands
should not be mistaken for divine
and only an abject fool declares himself immortal –
up to a point.

The gift finds you, you don't find it.


II.
I was late arriving at the poet's inaugural reading.
He was a good six poems in (not counting the haikus)
wheezing like a punctured tire through seven

lucky charm rhymes
broken window symbolism
the wheel as a great metaphor
you know, the usual stuff

pony bottle of sparkling mineral water
sweating at the podium
head down like a shamed Pomeranian
a shaved, sober monk in prayer.

His support group was there too –
fellow sweat shop poets
with self-inflicted haircuts and merlot coloured ascots
counting his syllables like sheep
nodding and smiling

# Sciamachy and Shell Roars

I.
imagining monastic defeat

what it takes to break this hermetic seal

sick of sciamachy

these thalidomide shadows that crutch waltz
on the ceilings fault line
around still bouquets of rust flowers
in and out of cobwebbed corners

malformed and malnourished

like those deep set wolf spider eyes
staring back from fuliginous mirrors
they charm the skin off of a diamondback
then flash fang its exposed throat

II.
you know

it's ok

to long for a stained glass worthy scene

a left handed portrait
that wobbles in its frame

that can't be explained

in pained, relative terms

or

a woman that blooms and bubble snaps
inside the heat mirage

her foil wings half unfolded
her star and barbed wire
five and dime diadem
could be a luminous nimbus
or a less elusive lucid dream
at first sight

III.
she offers a song
she hustled from a busker

a free avalanche ride

a predicate challenge to the night
with its peanut gallery of howler monkeys
and other shifty penumbral beings

if you wanted
a campfire cricket choir
you came to the wrong venue

this motley audience
eager to turn
eager to boo
eager to bruise
this reticent ingénue

a pregnant pause

a new magnetic ribbon on the trunk of an old cause

then she opens up her sparrow throat
unfurls her feathery tongue

and the voice comes soft,
susurrant,
it disarms
threatens to retard
after just a few silver-white notes

all the chairs were taken
I had to stand
there inside this austere café
where the paintings go to hang themselves
still wet
yet already up for sale
beside botanical teas and candied coffees
new age forever delayed.

He was struggling,
seemingly up on crutches
trying to be the next Lizard King
sans breathless wet leather
and/or mini-mart Dionysian decadence
hardly the new gelded Bukowski
the others were trying desperately to be.

He lived in a city
full of lacerating beauty
bright end of the night avenues
electric women with gazelle graces
and faces that once started ancient wars

yet his words were ugly, cold,
almost emotionless –
forced –
written for an audience rather than himself
it was embarrassing,
a cop out.

Then, at last, it was over.
No ketchup-grade tomatoes were thrown.

The support group clapped
the same soft, polite clap (spring rain golf delay)
they'd give Rimbaud, Morrison,
or some other feckless fraud
that writes cock odes at pained length
and/or sticky epistles
addressed to the back of some symmetrical sylph's kneecaps.

I got the hell out of there
before he could ask me what I thought
with his devouring eyes and need for validation
I just didn't have the heart

he was an alright kid after all
power hair/perfect teeth
an innocuous Aryan

never once got kicked in the ass
while on the ground
never once saw his mama
naked with a shiner
never once was rejected
by the same woman
thrice on the same night

he'd get asshole gaped
by the long hard truth in time
sans lubrication
some editors would find some use
for his tied tongue

a cub scout apple bobbing
in a Roman lion's den.

III.
Villon got it
so did Jeffers
the gift found them.

And Hem was right
when he said, and I paraphrase:
if you don't remember writing it
then it's worth keeping.

Hem probably remembered every syllable of
"Garden of Eden"

Now
about the *process*...

it's not painful,
if it is
you are probably forcing it

you'll give yourself a double hernia
or a prolapse that way

it's not child birth
it's not even an efficacious metaphor for it
(just ask your mother)

For me it's purity
that doe-eyed waif in the white dress
with the crystal skin and the good manners

before the dance, before the tears
and the bleeding, the regrets.

It is unmitigated joy,
the second greatest feeling
I have ever known.

Creation.

Watching the pen take my hand,
wondering what will come next...

hoping that it can be
at least half as poetic and beautiful
as my non-neurotic Siamese cat
stretching and yawning in a silver spot of moonlight
on that gracefully flawed Persian carpet

or...

seeing the woman I love

naked
in the morning glory blue light
just before dawn
breaks her golden yolk

she thinks I'm still sleeping

imagines me weightless, dreaming.

Soon the early songbirds shall raise their voices

explode into flight

eclipse all of this

as I open up my eyes.

# The Vision and the Void

*"I'll kindle my fires with the words
I can't send you
and the roads I can't follow
and the songs I can't sing"*

*~Townes Van Zandt*

## A Bullet for the Blind

this tenebrous tangle you call a tango
with smacked eyes at half-moon, half-mast,
sailing downward into these turbid puddles
a slurred second language
soon becomes a dead language
and you used to admire
your distorted reflection
in this puddle on clear and salient days
the way smiles are usually cut on a bias
occasionally sincere
so you do want to dance, don't you?
with pockets empty –
prolapsed and lop-eared –
whispering your poems as if they were incantations
and the music is just a tired grumble from your accumulated
mountain
the useless refuse you refuse to throw away
get down in the depression
and wait for the avalanche to cleanse you
purify you with purpose
the rain falls, for it has to,
finds you in the ditch, the mirror,
respect the echo's impact.

enter white Cecilia, exit black Mariah.

you see,
I've grown tired and restless
from these epics written by the elders
we've all been fed off the fat of them
and perhaps that's why they were permitted existence in the first
place
but it's no longer the dark ages, you say
we now have liposuction for these lines
we are no longer bullwhipped slaves to formalism, structure,
all obsequious smile and obeisant nod
then, my friend, my enemy,

why is the light so hard to find?
is it the eye full of spleen, left unsharpened,
or the tongue leaded with lye
soon to be swallowed?
if for nothing more
than a meager sustenance.

rue this day, its graveyard architecture, the storm it promises.

Oh, sweet Marie,
where are you tonight?
where are the six white horses you promised me?
in the penitentiary again
well it's better than the glue factory
Marie, is it still the same warden there,
the one that looks like Wilford Brimley?
will you tell him to set one horse free?
drag me out of this scene, quicksilver on the side of infinity,
trust me, I have reasons
and this night advances
bites like quicklime and erases identity
an ill-tempered silverback
that blows bows of blood into the air
rattles his own cage, demands soothing new age music
or the slow dazzling guts of last year's man
before they turn to dander.

hold this egg to the flame of your penny candle; now tell me, what do you see?

there's an elongated infant
with golden yolk quivering on his double chin
or is it the cloth spun from the sun's copulation?
he mistook his high chair for a throne
his flatulent voice calls for a coddle
a warm nipple and a diaper change
once cinched up
he temerariously lobs his obloquies
ignorant of the wind's true intentions
ignorant, too, of rudimentary physics

still there's queen-level drama in his princely court
in this diorama which of course is a self-portrait
where, with aid of prism imprisoned in his puckered anus
he shoots a rainbow for all to see
and several jesters with their Bosch ladybird dates
erupt triumphantly into montages of music.

Joni, was it the frayed heat or the hidden snake that made the
summer lawn hiss?

so, I put on my gloves
now my hands look brutal, like a storm
am I demon or dark horse?
am I messiah or white dove?
aren't we all
all of the above anyway?
talcum powdering our soft bums before climbing up on our
splintery crosses

so, I must become surgeon
without a single day of study
without a wall to hang my papers on
I must keep this instrument steady
even if the passing nurses
smile coquettishly and promise softer hells
each one floats by like a new Ophelia
like a bride without her daddy
trying to find the altar
with hands softer than the air she breathes.

after the amateurs are dissected
after a bloody beating heart is not detected
and last rites are written
I shall offer my writing hand to one of these brave new Ophelias
lead her down to the secreted ballroom
with its looking glass dancefloor
with its sea of swirling eyes
a vision and a void inside of each and every one
I shall show her the vaulted ceiling
painted with all the fiery colours of the womb

both sunset and swan in a slumberous lake
the single crack that occasionally lets some light in
and we'll dance,
with the graceful carelessness of children
until the ceiling fractures and falls
and the womb fucking wrecks it.

# The Vision and the Void

I.
I did not take to the image
of countless crippled christs
collapsing into a common pile
at the foot of the mountain

the sound of a small animal
caught in the brambles
straining to set herself free
remembering the scent
of her first kill

the sick geometry
of broken limbs
the sharp ache of those angles
shattered elbows
bursting kneecaps
sunken eyes and temples

*(where are these angels and their sweet songs
you claim to have heard on high?)*

the blackbirds that bloomed
and then flew out of
the open, often licked wounds

their infant eyes blind with salt
damn the whites of them
unfurled flaccid flags of surrender

the sky a matador's cape
red with the blood of another deflowering

the heart
so brutal and beautiful
a treasure, a curse,
buried in the bull

has stopped beating
the sword smeared with its
fierce colour of fire,
of passion,
sickly dripping –
dimming

and now the peasants
are throwing roses incautiously
with utter disregard for the thorns

singing songs
for sons of virgins
sons too soft for this slaughter

II.
In the mouth of this desert
I couldn't remember my name
or my horse's name
but I couldn't forget hers

the sand against my eye
every time she rain-bowed
all prismatic
through the dark prison
of my mind

for forty days
and forty nights

the Siamese sand
the colour of her skin

she removed her dress
shed her second skin
and it hung in the air
like breath in winter

and I knew I was alive

and that she was
a pure source of light
in these new dark ages

*(Gloria, in excelsis Dea)*

I was dry as that bony pile of christs
in that shadowy depression
at the foot of the mountain –
a hecatomb that pulsed with flies
the maggots dancing to the music
their own tiny bodies made
my horse's eyes, the light,
unwilling to touch that dark scene
which weaved shadows and spells –
cursed itself

but she was there
wasn't she?
if only for a moment in my mind
and I longed to drink
the water that surrounded her
the water on which she floated
in her crystal skiff
coruscating brightly as St. Elmo's fire

I longed to swim in her pools
in the languid light of her beauty reflected
caught in her blue wave
as honest as her silken web
running forever
half sick of shadows

she was Lady of Shalott
she was Lady of Lourdes
a monument of mercy
a holy mountain
if only for a fleeting moment

III.
a thirsty cripple in the mouth of a desert
his horse turning to glue
his heart screaming for the sword's swift release

trying to remember
where he buried that picture of his mother
mistaking the circling birds
that followed him
for a pious omen
confusing the mountain's strength
with his own

*(that holy mountain echoed no reply, no joyous strain)*


knowing all too well
the hours wasted inside that glass
blown and broken

he envied those birds
their wings perfect and weightless
their intentions both savage and pure

his eyes opened wide
as if to welcome them

for they had seen enough

the birds could have their way
with them now

as they stared in stillness –
upward –
beyond that silent mountain
in the direction of home

*(while our hearts in love we raise)*

# With This Ash We Polish Jewels

Shots ring out as shots are wont to
and right on cue the dogs start barking knives all at once.
You don't know if it's a siren, a scream, or a screaming siren's song
but it is just the way a cacophony should be –
it effectively coveys a cataclysm, a collapse –
like Jackson's veins, all substance scraped out of them;
like some eager poet's description of an implosion paradigm
and all of those other fresh hells, bread lines,
where daily attendance is deemed mandatory,
this, too, is non-negotiable.

Some nights you just get sick of the sky,
the slatternly stars and their winking striptease.
All the misunderstandings and questions
keep ringing in your neck
and you want to defenestrate yourself from the bell tower,
an elegant gesture of surrender;
one for all the crippled crows, the embers of past summers,
the weightless bright flights, and every other thing
you remember seeing in her eyes
when she got the mascara all wrong
and she looked beaten in the point blank mirror.

So you try to write out,
rather bleed out,
a dense history,
this time without hysterics;
fiercely forge yourself in purifying fire,
just lyrical enough to melt synapses
and unbridle the endorphins –
see how far you can lean without falling,
a precarious shadow of the person you once knew –
the hollow abandoned carapace
of the dream you once shared a splendid dependency with.
We've all brushed the ground from our faces,
we've all reached for that embalmed sky

in rolling blackout states, in fits of bruised vanity,
and, at our most desperate, in prayer.

Are the gazelles watching you with sliding electric eyes?
Their cellophane sighs filling your sails
as you make each new incision,
create Christ wounds that look like fruit
so ripe and feminine,
glistening and singing,
a brute choir assembled on your body.
Can you see them over there?
those gazelles, so plugged into that crystal blue current,
almost persuaded to leave the foxhole,
cross this narcotic distance,
catch an eyeful of your Roman candle rain,
your prismatic cumshot, your visionary Braille;
until you brandish that knife,
make it dance like Van's ballerina
and, size-wise, it's really nothing,
just a cautioning lady's finger
but, you see, there's this void reflected in it,
an ugly smudge across the grave face of the blade,
so, any advance would be pointless.
The gazelles just shake a little, then settle down,
with honeyed loins, with skin deliciously tender,
they wait for greater lions,
ok with just being meat.

Shots ring out because they have to.
And which idiot said the darkness can't be luminous?
Like a hunk of coal, it too can be broken,
and burned into fuel for perfect pentameter,
immortal verses, and reading rainbows –
several other truncated weapons and extended olive branches –
bible black hawks and pink-eyed doves
that coo the way rodeo sweethearts do,
over their dusty men's men and all of that bull.

Exquisite creatures with pretty mouths, riding pretty horses,
horses with shotgun legs,

that kick harder than the heart of this
and know when to run,
with the force and freedom of rivers,
both wild and true.

# Swing Low Sweet Pendulum

When her face is shaded in deep African violet such as this
I can hear her pores ripple; I listen to them screaming for distance
and I know her tongue is a cold fire
and I know if she tries to smile
it would surely destroy me
so I sever myself from the scene
and step outside.

First frost makes all the wires seem lower and more dangerous
it mutes all the orioles,
buries the tattered satin of their two-note songs
beneath the raw bosom of earth
distended orange bellies up
a watery sunrise painted by a motherless child
quickly dips back down into the ground.

And this freezing rain keeps falling
with a painless ambivalence I admire
and her pores keep screaming
of failures measured in fish scale
and stale green loaves of bread
even the scavengers avoid these scraps
cocooned in darkness,
yelping knives at animal midnight.

There was a time when the birds
shared the ground with her
relinquished their wings
as an offering to her
they nested in her hair
a wild and unattended spring
a triumph, a lush life,
waited in there –
a verdant surprise
ready to explode with newness.

The sky has a tense surface
it could be a body of water.

If she rises it's the same as falling
her bones so slow to shatter
the sound her only remainder
yes, it is a song
unfit for western ears.

From the outside
the façade of this house, our home,
seems softened, warm and inviting
the windows glow morning orange
indifferent to the restlessness,
the recurring haunting and unremitting storm –
oh to know the kind blindness of those windows!

What I know, I'd rather forget.
She's just another kingdom of rain
waiting for me inside the cold heart of that home;
if there is a place past this blue, I haven't found it yet.

I hope to find her sleeping
cradled, as she should be, in her saturnine shawl.
I hope to find some luminous logic
in the bottle of liquor I've kept hidden from her
so that when she shakes herself free from this slumber
my eyes look different, softer,
so that when she smiles, this time with ease,
she sees herself in these honest eyes,
realizes she's just another part of me,
as I am of her, one and the same.

The cycle breaks, makes a beautiful sound,
our indigo moods finally find stability on the trapeze
no more violet/violent vicissitudes in this sky or sea –
one and the same to the neophytic night pilot,
and we make our first down payment on a brighter flight
into the tremulous heart of new tomorrow's sun.

for then I wouldn't fear lapidification –

and all of those perverted little Pygmalionists –

with their attempted molestaches…

that swarm of bees beneath the mirror,

or was it my eyes

with you in them?

and all of that window to the soul bullshit –

honey brained infancy

a fantasy of fucking myself

just to feel better, or something.

I'm sorry,

you are not some insecurity

projected inside-out from me

a Gordian knot to cleave

with a knife once used

to cut sugar cookies in the shape of evergreens

and/or

sucking wounds in the shape of David's stars

no

you are more a ball-peen hammer

loosed in the blood –

a constructive melancholy

that understands the necessity

of succinct suicide notes,

reading fortunes in the margins.

there are saviors with wounds out there, you know,

wounds that sing like musical saws

wounds that smell like lilac wine

all inside out in eggshell negative space, so vague,

so sterile and white, too white to be safe –

the second mind lives

as it suckles the Milky Way,

it's a tiger's teat

pink as untested infant skin,

conjunctivitis,

all those sick notes –

you know, they made the perfect song –

the correct sunset for that dangling swan.

I want you to know,

your paintings still eviscerate me –

pull my beating heart out through my anus,

and if that isn't genius,

I don't know what the hell is.

## Minor Keys and Places

I.
daguerreotypes on the inside of a purple eyelid
hanging heavy – cockeyed
unattended tenement shade
(they call them efficiencies these days)

there's just enough space
a tiny seam
a little light
you can see limpid green

remember the irreversible sadness of that eye
you could bugger a fat unabridged dictionary
for the better part of a lonely night
beneath Waits' grapefruit moon and solitary star
and never find the right word
for that sadness, that eye,
a word that would preserve, rather than disfigure,
the moment and its rich discovery.

II.
if you could salvage a well-tuned,
wild blue piano from these beautiful ruins
then play it with your mongoloid fingers
fingers that can't seem to do anything right but write
you can paint a scene
not in black and white
rather a dull human gray

see her shitfaced on human kindness
with all the sudden sweetness
and subtle burn of good blended whiskey
she's drinking brandy at the bright end of the bar
the same eye, this time without bruise, just like the other
soft and wide open, sailing –
at mach speed towards the unforgiving rocks

eyes of a siren that couldn't stop singing
her salty shattered dog tongue, fit to be tied –
and that inevitable crash
it always makes such a beautiful sound.

III.
the same wind that once cried wolf, cried Mary,
now screams her name
this wind once pushed by her dream
her dance, her body –
like frayed white heat,
a trap in the mirage

now it's just a pale surrender flag
torn and pathetically flapping
the stupid sound of one hand clapping
soon to be muted and consumed
conquered by this

the sky's incestuous gut
howls at the sun for it

the wind can't cry anymore
still it remembers her name
but her face cannot be placed

that tiny purple eyelid
all the distended dreams beneath it
like birds trapped indoors
flying into closed windows
(they know no window)

this sensation of glass shattering in chest
some things are better left unsaid

*try to forget.*

try to forget.

# The Weight of Human Stain on Wing

*for C.*

she appears as flashing x-ray first
clearly defined fault lines
a few fractures to finger

scarecrow silhouette
trembling shadow
overexposed

tragic arrows fly
criss-crossing birds
slow sizzling neon signs point

she knows where this is going

eyes at half-moon
under morphine drip purple lids
a vase of bruised irises
crooked heliotrope halo

all of it somehow right
against the slanted slate sky
set so low
waiting to be engraved
with sharp elegiac words
the kind designed to tug at entrails

the score: violin violence

\*     \*     \*

distended koala face
still pretty
she hopes
still kissable

pretty as the dixie peach promenade
or whatever it was daddy used to say

for something like a second
sunlight strains through silk

only to be poached
trapped and skinned
hung in abattoir darkness
a sad empty trophy

the love star on her wrist
a death's head in this light

the mirror waits
a black hole threshold
savage gravity
graceless frame

\*       \*       \*

she remembers
his hands cradling horseleg shotgun
crushing the breast of spring's first robin
turning soil prematurely
hopefully tethered together now
by fire-forged steel that bites into skin

that seems about right

she knows love
real love
and it's not bull and china
bulldozer and field of daisies

convenience store roses
and a carton of smokes

rhyming poetry
and a heart shaped card

just to say he's sorry

there's sorrow deep in the marrow of this —
she knows it -

the way he has serial maimed her spirit
extinguished the last gleaming wish

\*     \*     \*

the sound of blades
sharpening themselves against stone
out in the naked negative space
between her bones and home

can't ignore the portents anymore
the fatal echoes
the circle games
and certain cycles

life as last chapter
in a southern gothic novel

she could take a straight razor to every page
and still not silence the Wilhelm scream
rising in her blood

she could let tragic dimensions fester

blister

balloon

burst

with yellow ribbons
long black veils
passing trains
wind songs
and rain dances

or just let go

pack the suitcase
lipstick a message
feed the cat
take a silkwood shower
burn the pictures
the letters
the stillborn dream
the whistling ghosts

watch the flames crest
with distinguished fury

hear it all
snap hiss and pop

until everything is seared clean

then call daddy
and talk about it all
on the drive back home

the warm gold
of the country a.m. radio
and the cool six gun on his hip

making perfect sense again
in the safe wake of his smile
breaking like a brand new day

in the soft heart of his embrace
where broken things are mended

forgiven
and redeemed.

## High Society

A parliament of owls
presides over this night
reading the line of quick glowing eyes
fiery with life, the love of it.

Out loud it all sounds like a riot act being silenced
or a white church full of candles being blown out.

The cautious movements of the moon grazers –
old classical music played by precocious neophytes,
quick-study greenhorns –
see they live on the ground, off of the ground,
a place much closer to death,
which they don't really fear
for they know it is just a slight change.

They are good listeners.
When they hear the branches snapping
along with the wind's high harmony
it sounds like real bad juju doo-wop
without the benefit of light from the hangman's lantern
or a magnetic chorus designed to pull bodies together
no, this is just a slow dance with target range silhouettes
and now it's time to move or bust.

The owls descend in calm, stately shadows
breaking with easy grace and danger
a hand never seen
until it strikes
and the precious vessel drips red
with lost innocence and sick, waxing luster.

And why didn't winter
warn you to stay underground?
she's so white, so cryptic,
sterile as milk from the night nurse's breast
though hardly as safe.

That urge for going
isn't that what drove you beneath the earth in the first place?
chambered you in warm, rich layers of recombinant dream
despite starless ceiling
or moon to foment the rising blood into song.

A golden place to rest your weary legs
and catch your breath
when the heart feels lonely and hunted
wrongfully accused
for this night warns sun to stay away
until all spells and crimes
are documented and concealed
embossed and sealed
by the cold chill of time.

This parliament of owls
with dark appetites,
rapacious and insatiable
they hide inside one dollar bills
in N. California forests
where the tallest trees have been sighing deeply forever
for they know the pellets of this parliament
hide a terrible tangle of secrets
these owls have eyes all over the sky,
inside of everything, everywhere,
they burn slow spreading cancer,
and never dance with their masks off.

# Weakness or Obstacle.

this morning the light slants anxious

it shivers with a sickness

known in albatross and in syphilis

all fool's gold and bitter brittle blue

it suggests a familiar scene

a weakness or an obstacle

a vainglorious tourist sorely missing sleep


I squint my eyes

and I could be Lee Van Cleef

and in this (I want to call it national park) light

you appear as stranger

then heat mirage

then goddess (with velvet alms for paupers in her pocket)

then, finally, March hare

wild and naked in your newness

your incongruous beauty

appears as calamity

to the untrained eye

something's been pilfered

from the quicksilver cloud of this dream

and the thrill of the unfamiliar you

well,

it plays my spine marimba with virtuosity

turns my heart into honeycomb

honeybees buzzing in illuminated hollows

inside the eyes of everything

beneath vanity mirrors you made famous

until they were turned off

in the presence of your absence


then you turn towards me

deciduous sunlight shatters

into cold dagger

flashing snowblind eyes

wide open

wide shut

stinging with the familiar –

the certain flaws and useless songs

we worshipped long ago

before the pretty words

disfigured the lie

that was just beautiful enough

to live in.

# Not Long for This World

Spanish gold and lambent skin

remain true when eye teeth bite

when the blood's crescendo

can no longer retard

after the last charade is played

the last martyr slain

for seeing only what he owned

and all the sequined fans fall


treat it like a wheat penny

make your little MGM wish

now throw it down the well

brief candles

a broken eye

her broken body

the birds watch

but know better than to follow

open beaks full of refuse

which they'll weave into a nest

a sacred thing

how is this not alchemy?


this broken birth

your tender throat

swells with screams

for a hasty re-entry

a soft confinement

where the walls won't whisper

tasteless traducements –

both founded and unfounded –

for now


cancel all tongues

fry them in the lard

sucked from his latest epic

plug each conquistador's restless arquebus

with your long white writer's fingers

safe as mother's milk

they too sought glory and definition

all too quickly

hastened their own demise


dissolve these descending dreams

still bright as deciduous sunlight

warm and favonian

on winter's skin

a guileless virgin's hope

the yolk's been broken over easy

the torn flower an otiose garnish


time to piss up your own noose

let her be the chair you kick away

Spanish gold that never loses its luster

and her skin not porcelain or alabaster

just lambent

she's a graceful description of light

a ballet of braille for the blind

this beauty touches them too

please Chopin,

stop chasing that fille de joie –

she'll never sew your wounds closed –

because we need another scherzo

we need to know your zal

learn how to evoke it

the groundswell of honest emotion

brighten the black – the mood, the night, the void within us –

yes all of us – and the dream

running like a filmstrip beneath us –

beneath everything


please Rimbaud,

clear your throat of Verlaine's semen

just long enough to read one line true

in a voice that ignites plasma

splatter it across the naïve face of this

you know this poetry game

is the softest racket in town

and the highway is all spread out

like a free-spirited woman before us

flaming like another Rome

with not a single violin string

to tie her world to.

## To Catch and Cradle His Crown

*a proper coronach for Casey*

It was a weary dream

one I was content to be pulled from

if only by your voice, always true,

calling out for me

in threnodic tones

in stertorous breath

a tragic telepathy


in time to find

your body still warm

your once strong legs failing

some light still pulsing,

a pure source,

inside your eyes

retreating to brilliant corners

where it dripped its honey

into the bitter encroaching darkness

several shades

several blades

of gray

in muted flash

in drifting fade

shadow and snow

your breath so slow to rise

your spirit touching me

again.


the sky closer than ever before

indifferent as always

tenebrous and restless

I wanted to reach up

raise my hand in a gesture of surrender

soft as tired eyes slowly closing

sweetly yielding to sleep

that sky

so close

that we could reach inside

feel its guts

so much softer than our own

all feather and dander

the womb from which this wayward dream descended.


oh, we are stronger than this

our bond is bolder

tested centuries ago, now tested again

in biased rising flame

in sinking kingdoms of rain

in the savage shadow of arrows

slung by heartless hunters

a place where

even the mockingbirds go silent


we heard the ringing snap

of the patient trap

always waiting to tear us apart –

to smile through our blood –

with which it cravenly masks itself

howling sadly through the air we breathed

the day we shared

together

side by side

far ahead of any sunset

or wounded horizon.


I held you in my arms

wanted to give you my health, my breath

watched the shutter fall on 10,000 films of happiness

all rain on lens

blurring the frame

but not before

seeing you on that clear summer day

leaping and loping

through soft blades of grass

which the wind made whisper

with her sweet breath

you gracefully lacing

in and out of pillars of sunlight

which your bright eyes eclipsed

reflecting their own light

unbroken symbols of purity

untouched treasure

we were there together

sharing the same spirit


I felt this

wanted to replay every single frame

find ineffable beauty in every pause

as I held you in my arms.


I caught your falling crown

wouldn't let it touch the ground

which was too cold to cradle it

or compose a proper coronach for it.


I watched your feet kick

as if to push back the darkness

or maybe you were already loping

through those fields

we used to run together

over several lifetimes

with joy in our hearts

with beauty in our bones


ignited eyes


and death was just a

a baying bloodhound

a famished fox

a heartless hunter

a diminishing dot

in the safe distance.


In time, my friend

I too, shall follow

and catch you

before the sad wind can

on legs weightless

and heartbreakingly new.

## In Connection With a Drowning

in legion with this early darkness

a blanket of smallpox

covering the anemic winter skin

crisp as a leper's

this newness you swoon for

and celebrate prematurely

it breeds disquietude

amends lines once improvised

callow hands that never once

handled something frangible

without breaking it

the ice cold crystal shatter

a fault line of blue

on the lake's ceiling

a tragic swirl of swan's eye and frigid star

glittering like errors

a tiny breath still hanging in the air

the message dissipates in drifting surrender

and the child is long gone.

# Epilogue

## Tasmanian Persecution

scythe in dander gut of sky
too weak to push air
the way dreams often do
more bayonet than butterfly

a noble species lies down
and weeps for all that is wrong
with this human stain
their innate penchant for destruction

their prisons of measured time
their conflicted religions
the way they trap themselves
the way they find blindness
and stay there

bright animal eyes
see beyond
this arrogance
these conceits

blood, heartbeat,
breath, cum;
the light and privilege
of dreams

the only true gods
are on the inside

honey in the hollows
of the body at rest
golden, flowing freely
when in motion

eyes sharp and honest
even when they are closing forever
howling to be free
on the bruised lip
of this insatiable void

no more crepuscular hunts
for the Thylacine
that tiger couldn't be saved

the poachers came
with sport and bloodlust
with bounty avarice

stinking of cheap tobacco
rotgut rye and gunpowder

raping nature
without compunction

£1 per head for dead adults
and ten shillings for pups
2,184 bounties paid

the last captive Thylacine
never had a chance to run

they named her Benjamin
she died of starvation
and criminal neglect
in some godforsaken
Tasmanian zoo

a few photographs survive
a short black and white reel
reveals a creature
rare and magnificent
pacing and impatient

a snuff film of the spirit
as it leans toward
the unyielding shadows
of a certain extinction

the last tiger lies down
in cold, cramped quarters exposed
a beautiful creature dies

without the benefit
of a place to hide
from a row of obdurate eyes
human, heartless, and ignoble.

# Permissions & Acknowledgements

**A medallion level thank you to:**

Michael Crawford, Joanne Crawford, William Crawford Sr., Grace Paynter, Roberta Schlagel, Lou Schlagel, Lilia Meehan, Soul Sister Sadie, Brother Casey, Vivian Hesse, Shelly Sims, Steve Cleary, Bob Craig, Rick Gator, Timothy Reifsnyder, Jessica "Coop" Cooney, Frank Volpe, Mike English, Dale Winslow, Cathleen Daly, Walt Burns, Frank Reardon, April Michelle Bratten, Zoë Miller, Jillian Parker, Donna Snyder, Jacqui Corcoran, John Cassavetes, and the Persian carpet makers.

**Special thanks to the editors of the following publications in which some of these poems have previously appeared:**

*Sugar Mule, Counterexample Poetics, Calliope Nerve, Unlikely 2.0, Leaf Garden Press, Up the Staircase Quarterly, and Differentia Press.*

# About the Author

photo by Kimberly Schlagel

**William Crawford** has been nominated for a Pushcart Prize in poetry. His work has appeared in numerous magazines and anthologies, most recently including, *Counterexample Poetics, The Criterion, Danse Macabre, Differentia Press: Corporeal Manifestations, Unlikely Stories of the Third Kind, Leaf Garden, Luciole Press,* and *Up the Staircase Quarterly.* **Fire in the Marrow** is his first poetry collection. William lives in Philadelphia, Pennsylvania, and is an animal rights activist.

NeoPoiesis
a new way of making


in ancient Greece, poiesis referred to the process of making
creation – production – organization – formation – causation
a process that can be physical and spiritual
biological and intellectual
artistic and technological
material and teleological
efficient and formal
a means of modifying the environment
and a method of organizing the self
the making of art and music and poetry
the fashioning of memory and history and philosophy
the construction of perception and expression and reality


NeoPoiesis Press
reflecting the creative drive and spirit
of the new electronic media environment

www.ingramcontent.com/pod-product-compliance
Lightning Source LLC
Chambersburg PA
CBHW022007100426
42738CB00041B/727